Isaac Asimov's

21st Century

Library of the
Universe

Near and Far

Comets and Meteors

BY ISAAC ASIMOV

WITH REVISIONS AND UPDATING BY RICHARD HANTULA

Gareth Stevens Publishing
A WORLD ALMANAC EDUCATION GROUP COMPANY

Please visit our web site at: www.garethstevens.com
For a free color catalog describing Gareth Stevens Publishing's list of high-quality
books and multimedia programs, call 1-800-542-2595 (USA) or 1-800-387-3178 (Canada).
Gareth Stevens Publishing's fax: (414) 332-3567.

Library of Congress Cataloging-in-Publication Data

Asimov, Isaac.
    Comets and meteors / by Isaac Asimov; with revisions and updating by Richard Hantula.
        p. cm. – (Isaac Asimov's 21st century library of the universe. Near and far)
    Includes bibliographical references and index.
    ISBN 0-8368-3966-8 (lib. bdg.)
    1. Comets–Juvenile literature. 2. Meteors–Juvenile literature. I. Hantula, Richard.
    II. Asimov, Isaac. Discovering comets and meteors. III. Title.
    QB721.5.A832 2005
    523.6–dc22   2004058940

This edition first published in 2005 by
Gareth Stevens Publishing
A WRC Media Company
330 West Olive Street, Suite 100
Milwaukee, WI 53212 USA

Revised and updated edition © 2005 by Gareth Stevens, Inc. Original edition published in 1990
by Gareth Stevens, Inc. under the title *Comets and Meteors*. Second edition published in 1996
by Gareth Stevens, Inc. under the title *Discovering Comets and Meteors*. Text © 2005 by
Nightfall, Inc. End matter and revisions © 2005 by Gareth Stevens, Inc.

Series editor: Mark J. Sachner
Cover design and layout adaptation: Melissa Valuch
Picture research: Matthew Groshek
Additional picture research: Diane Laska-Swanke
Production director: Jessica Morris

The editors at Gareth Stevens Publishing have selected science author Richard Hantula to bring
this classic series of young people's information books up to date. Richard Hantula has written
and edited books and articles on science and technology for more than two decades. He was
the senior U.S. editor for the *Macmillan Encyclopedia of Science*.

In addition to Hantula's contribution to this most recent edition, the editors would like to
acknowledge the participation of two noted science authors, Greg Walz-Chojnacki and
Francis Reddy, as contributors to earlier editions of this work.

Printed in the United States of America

1 2 3 4 5 6 7 8 9 09 08 07 06 05

Contents

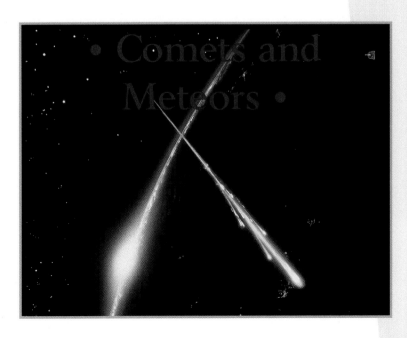

We live in an enormously large place – the Universe. It's only natural that we would want to understand this place, so scientists and engineers have developed instruments and spacecraft that have told us far more about the Universe than we could possibly imagine.

We have seen planets up close, and spacecraft have even landed on some. We have learned about quasars and pulsars, supernovas and colliding galaxies, and black holes and dark matter. We have gathered amazing data about how the Universe may have come into being and how it may end. Nothing could be more astonishing.

Some celestial bodies have been known since very ancient times. Early peoples saw comets in the sky and wondered about them, and were often terrified by them. "Shooting stars," or meteors, were also seen in ancient times. Some people thought meteors were stars that had come loose from the heavens and fallen. How surprised they would have been to learn the truth about comets and meteors that scientific study has provided.

Comet Ikeya-Seki, one of the very brighest comets to appear in the twentieth century, photographed in the early morning sky near Tucson, Arizona, in 1965.

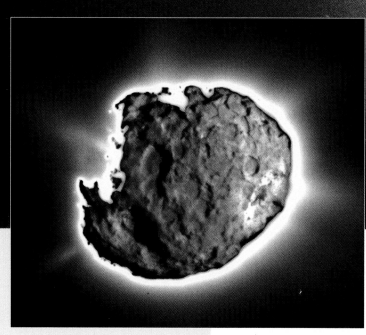

Right: Comet Wild-2, photographed by the space probe *Stardust* in 2004. The image was processed to show the streams of gas and dust coming from the comet's surface.

Hazy to Bright

A comet can look like just a hazy patch in the sky. It is made of ice, rock, and dust and appears as a very dim haze at the start. Then it slowly moves among the stars from night to night, getting brighter, then fading again until it disappears.

The hazy patch stretches out into a "tail" that always points away from the direction of the Sun. The tail gets longer as the comet grows brighter, until it sometimes stretches far across the sky. Then the tail shortens and fades.

Ancient peoples imagined a comet as a person's head with long hair streaming behind. In fact, the word *comet* comes from a Greek word meaning "hair."

Above: A woman's head with long hair streaming behind was a favorite image of a comet.

Spectacular Comets

Comets come in a variety of sizes and shapes. Some can be quite large. In 1811, a huge comet appeared in the sky. Its head was a cloud of dust that was said to be larger than the Sun; its tail stretched for millions of miles.

Other notable large comets showed up in 1861 and 1882, and Halley's Comet made a spectacular appearance in 1910. Comet Hyakutake in 1996 sported a dazzlingly long tail, and Comet Hale-Bopp was a dramatic sight in the sky for much of 1997.

Remarkable close-up pictures of comets have been taken by spacecraft such as NASA's *Stardust* and the European Space Agency's *Rosetta*. *Rosetta*, which was launched in 2004, is carrying a lander that is supposed to land on a comet called Churyumov-Gerasimenko in 2014.

Comet Hale-Bopp in 1997.

What makes a comet flop?

Sometimes astronomers are fooled into thinking a far-off comet is a large one. Because Comet Kohoutek was seen far off in 1973, it was expected to be a huge, bright comet. It turned out not to be. On the other hand, Comet West, from which little was expected when it was discovered in 1975, turned out to be quite bright. A thick, rocky crust might be one reason why a comet looks duller than expected as it nears the Sun.

Some of history's spectacular comets include Donati's Comet in 1858 over Paris, France (*above*), and Comet Seki-Lines in 1962 (*left*).

Like Clockwork — Halley's Comet

After Sir Isaac Newton developed the Law of Gravity in 1687, his friend Edmond Halley became fascinated with comets. In 1682 a comet had crossed the sky, following the same path as comets in 1531 and 1607. Using the Law of Gravity, Halley showed that what was thought of as three different comets was actually the same comet traveling around the Sun in a long orbit and returning about every 75 to 76 years. He predicted that the comet would return in 1758 and would take its usual path across the sky. In 1759 the comet came back; it was a little late because Jupiter's strong gravity slowed it down.

The comet has since been known as Halley's Comet. It also returned in 1835, in 1910, and in 1986, when it was photographed by spacecraft.

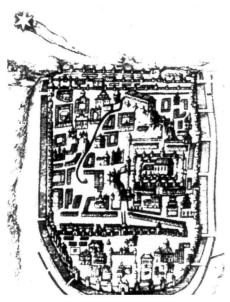

Above: A sketch from the seventeenth century of Halley's Comet in the skies.

Above: A close-up of Halley's Comet compiled from images made by the space probe *Giotto* in 1986.

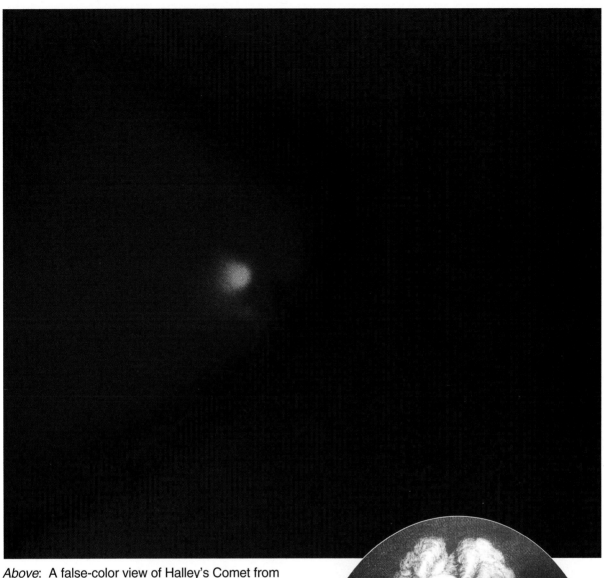

Above: A false-color view of Halley's Comet from the European Space Agency's 1986 *Giotto* mission. *Giotto* took the first pictures of a comet ever made from an extremely close distance.

Right: Edmond Halley, the English astronomer who was the first to predict a comet's return.

Nothing More than Dust

Before Edmond Halley determined the orbits of comets, many people thought comets were warnings of upcoming horrible events on Earth. Because a comet's tail could look like the hair of a wailing woman, or like a sword, the occurrence of a comet was thought to be a sign of war or some other disaster. When a large comet appeared, crowds of people would pray and church bells would ring.

Even in fairly recent periods, people have panicked over comets. In 1910, Earth passed through the tail of Halley's Comet. At the time, many people were afraid this meant the world was going to come to an end.

The tail of Halley's Comet, however, like that of every other comet, is made of just dust and gas, and nothing more.

Right: A humorous and historic look at a grim thought – a comet destroys Earth, while the Man in the Moon smiles on.

Comets — a prediction of doom?

Halley's Comet appeared in A.D. 66, a year that saw the Jews launch a revolt against Rome; four years later, the Temple in Jerusalem was destroyed. Halley's Comet appeared in 1066, and the Saxons of England were defeated by William the Conqueror. The comet appeared in 1456, and the Turks mopped up the very last bits of the Roman Empire. It seems as if whenever a comet appears, there is some sort of war, death, or other disaster. But that doesn't mean the comet is connected with the event. After all, terrible events also occur whenever a comet does not appear.

In Paris in 1811, many people were afraid that comets would bring disaster.

Right: Montezuma, ruler of the Aztecs, is shown being frightened by a comet in 1520.

The Kuiper Belt

The Kuiper Belt is a region of the Solar System that begins around the orbit of the planet Neptune and extends outward for a considerable distance beyond the orbit of Pluto. It contains thousands upon thousands of icy and rocky objects. The belt is named for the American astronomer Gerard Kuiper, who predicted its existence. Scientists discovered the first Kuiper Belt objects in the 1990s.

Some Kuiper Belt objects, such as Quaoar, are bigger than the largest asteroids. But many smaller objects in the belt are probably icy comets. In fact, the Kuiper Belt seems to be the source of most comets that take less than 200 years to orbit the Sun. Even comets traveling in very short orbits around the Sun may have originally come from the Kuiper Belt.

The objects known as centaurs may also have originated in the Kuiper Belt. These few objects resemble asteroids in some ways but orbit the Sun in the region between Jupiter and Neptune. The first centaur to be discovered was Chiron, in 1977. It was found to have a coma – the cloud of dust and gas that surrounds the core of a comet. If Chiron really is a comet and if it is someday knocked into an orbit making it easily visible from Earth, it might create a truly breathtaking sight in the sky. Scientists think it may up to 125 miles (200 km) across – or around twenty times bigger than Halley's Comet.

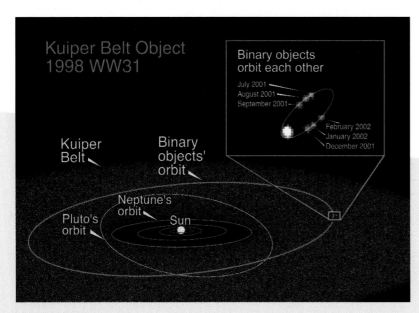

Left: The Kuiper Belt object known as 1998 WW31 (it was discovered in 1998) turned out to be a "binary" system consisting of two objects that orbit around each other!

This illustration shows an artist's idea of spectacular eruptions on Chiron as it passes Saturn. Chiron takes about 50 years to orbit the Sun.

Right: An artist's conception of the large Kuiper Belt object called Quaoar, believed to be half the size of Pluto.

13

The Oort Cloud

Not all comets that we see from Earth originate in the Kuiper Belt. Some seem to come from far, far away, following paths that may not bring them back for thousands or millions of years. Astronomers believe that such "long-period" comets come from a huge collection of billions or even trillions of icy comets that may lie tens of thousands of times farther out from the Sun than Earth. This cloud of comets surrounds the rest of the Solar System. It is named for Dutch astronomer Jan Oort, who came up with the idea for it in 1950.

Comets from the Oort Cloud "fall" toward the Sun when their orbits are disturbed by a passing star or when they collide with each other. Such comets ordinarily travel in orbits around the Sun that may take millions of years to complete.

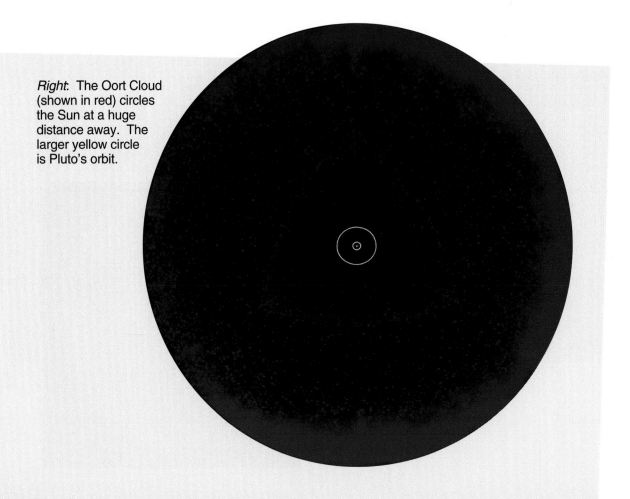

Right: The Oort Cloud (shown in red) circles the Sun at a huge distance away. The larger yellow circle is Pluto's orbit.

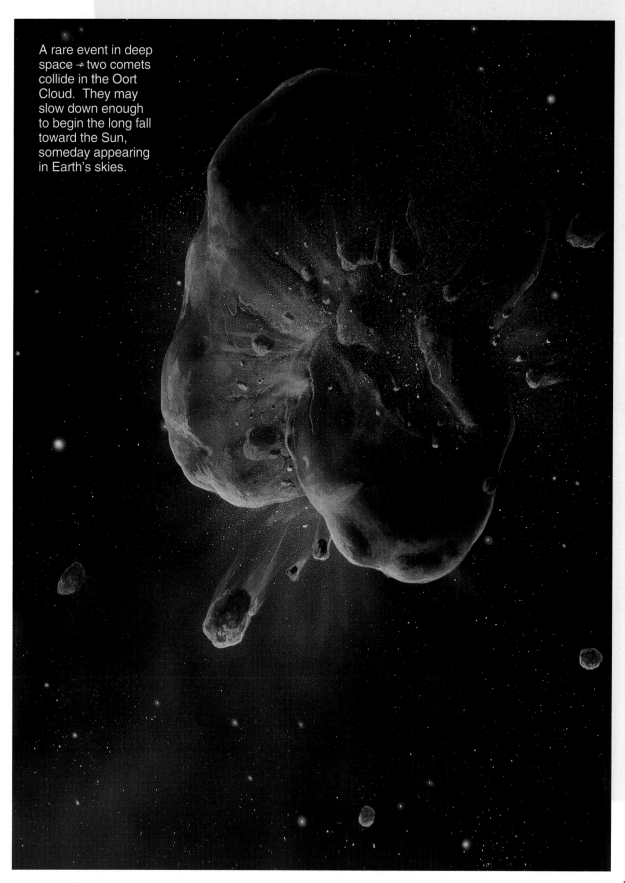

A rare event in deep space — two comets collide in the Oort Cloud. They may slow down enough to begin the long fall toward the Sun, someday appearing in Earth's skies.

15

"Shooting Stars" – Meteors

Like comets, meteors have fascinated and frightened people for centuries. Meteors look like stars that shoot across the sky for a distance and then disappear. The word *meteor* comes from the Greek words meaning "things in the air." And, indeed, meteors are shining objects that streak through Earth's atmosphere.

In areas where there are no city lights to interfere with your view of the sky, such "shooting stars" can be seen on almost any clear, moonless night, especially after midnight. Sometimes dozens are visible in a single night. Usually, meteors are quite dim, but sometimes they are bright enough to be called "fireballs."

But meteors are not really stars. Real stars always stay in the sky, no matter how many "shooting stars" streak across the heavens!

Right: A scientist studies a possible meteorite from Mars that was found in the Antarctic.

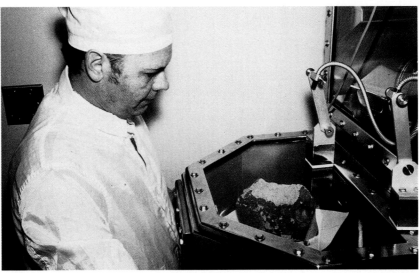

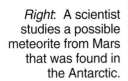

Meteorites – really Moon and Mars rocks?

Some meteorites contain the same materials - and the same proportion of materials - that make up Moon rocks. When asteroids and large meteorites bombarded the Moon and gouged out craters there, the Moon's weak gravity allowed some of the material to be knocked off its surface. Thus, some of the meteorites found on Earth are actually Moon rocks. There are also Mars rocks on Earth - a few meteorites have been found that include gases with the make-up of the Martian atmosphere.

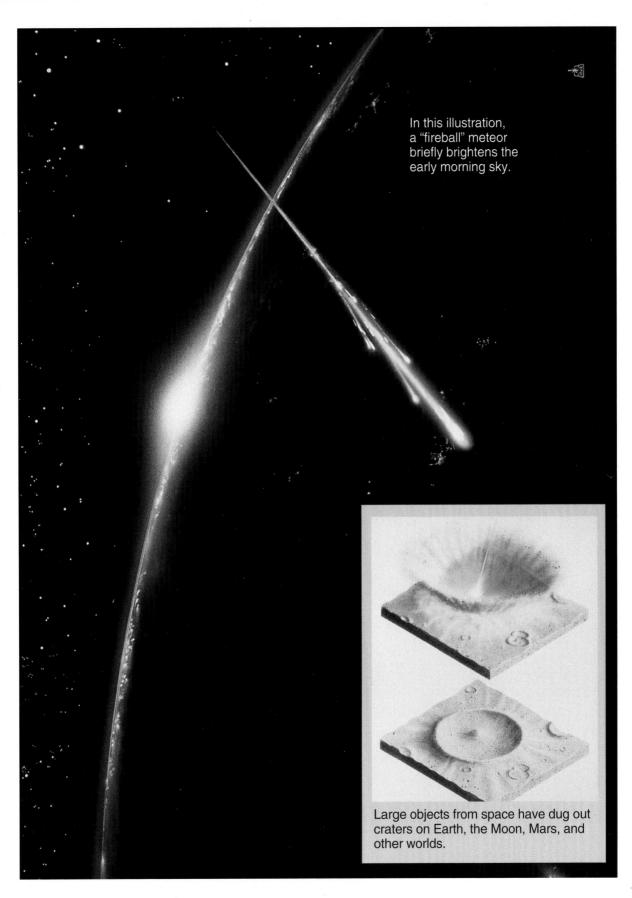

In this illustration, a "fireball" meteor briefly brightens the early morning sky.

Large objects from space have dug out craters on Earth, the Moon, Mars, and other worlds.

The remains of a burned-out comet. Particles of dust and rock trail along its orbit and eventually become meteors when Earth passes through the comet's path.

It's Raining Meteors!

Comets and certain kinds of meteors are related. That is because icy comets contain countless particles of dust and rock. When a comet's orbit takes it nearer the Sun's heat, some of the ice evaporates, freeing bits of dust and rock along with gases and forming the comet's coma and tail. Particles of material drift away from the comet but continue to orbit the Sun. Over millions of years the particles spread out along the comet's orbit, making it a band of dust.

Earth passes through several such bands each year. When Earth's atmosphere sweeps up the dust, the particles pass rapidly through the air. As a result of friction with the atmosphere, they heat up, become white hot, and glow. People on Earth see this as a "meteor shower."

In major showers such as the Perseids in August and the Leonids in November, up to dozens of meteors, or more, can be seen each hour.

Right: A photo of the Leonid meteor shower streaking through Earth's atmosphere. The Leonid shower occurs every year, but it tends to be exceptionally heavy every 33 years. The latest heavy shower was in 1999, so the next one should occur in 2032.

Meteors, Meteoroids, and Meteorites

Not all meteors are caused by comet dust. Many are caused by chunks of rock or small asteroid-like objects made of rock and metal that enter Earth's atmosphere from space. While they are speeding through space, such objects are called meteoroids. When a meteoroid strikes Earth's atmosphere and becomes white hot, it is called a meteor.

Most meteors are tiny objects and heat up enough to turn entirely into vapor. But some are too large to burn up completely. Bits of them survive and reach Earth's surface. These pieces are called meteorites.

Above: Pictured is a slice through a meteorite. Only the outer crust is affected by its fiery fall to Earth. The rest of the rock provides scientists with clues about the early days of our Solar System.

Finding meteorites!

Unless you see a meteorite actually fall, you're not likely to find one just by looking on the ground. Most look too much like ordinary rocks. However, in the Arctic and Antarctic regions of Earth, with their large, remote, ice-covered surfaces, a piece of rock on top of the ice would just about have to be a meteorite. There's really no other way it could have gotten there!

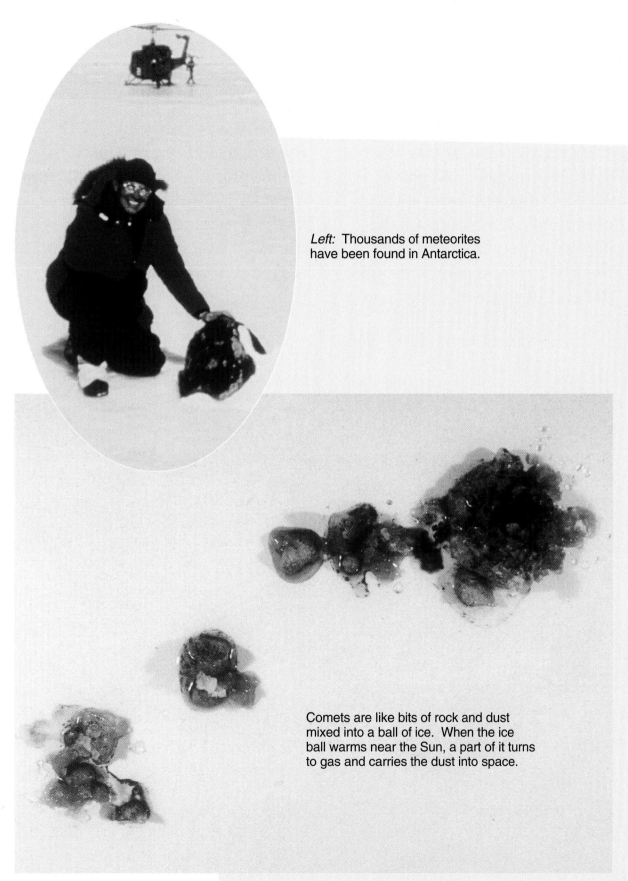

Left: Thousands of meteorites have been found in Antarctica.

Comets are like bits of rock and dust mixed into a ball of ice. When the ice ball warms near the Sun, a part of it turns to gas and carries the dust into space.

The Sky Is Falling!

Reports of meteor sightings weren't always taken seriously. In 1833, Earth passed through a huge collection of tiny dust particles in space. As many as 200,000 meteors were seen in one night! It was one of the biggest meteor showers ever reported. Some people thought the end of the world was coming.

Many scientists at that time believed that meteors were in some way connected with the weather or were caused by something on Earth. But all the meteors in the shower seemed to come from the same part of the sky. This fact helped people realize that meteors *could* fall from the sky.

Above: The great meteor shower of 1833 is seen from Niagara Falls in this historic drawing.

This illustration shows a unique location for observing a meteor shower – from a balloon!

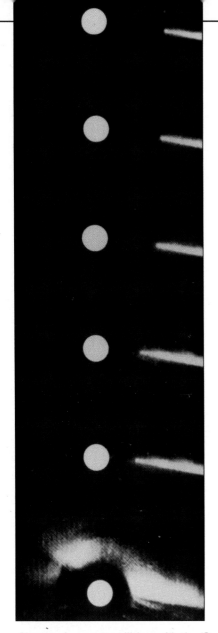

Comets Vanishing

Meteor showers contain material a comet has lost forever. With each trip near the Sun, a comet loses more material. Over the years, the comet shrinks. After a few hundred or thousand orbits, all its icy material is gone.

The rocky core that remains may resemble little more than a small asteroid sailing through the cosmos. If there is no rocky core, the comet vanishes completely and leaves nothing but a cloud of dust and rock bits.

Occasionally, though, a comet will die in a more spectacular way. In July 1994 a comet crashed into Jupiter, creating some of the most spectacular celestial fireworks ever seen!

Above: A comet collides with the Sun in this sequence of photos taken from space in 1979. Comet Howard-Koomen-Michels is shown racing closer to the Sun. Only a cloud of dust and gas emerges from the Sun's other side.

Kamikaze comets?

Some comets pass so close to the Sun that they skim only 1 million miles (1.6 million km) or less above its surface. The Sun's heat is enough to break the comets into a string of four or five fragments. These may skim by the Sun on their return visit, like beads on a necklace. Astronomers have even seen comets plunge into the Sun.

Because of the heat of the Sun, this comet's ice is turning to gas, and a faint tail has begun to form.

In 1994, Comet Shoemaker-Levy 9 was broken into pieces by Jupiter's gravity. It then smashed into the giant planet.

Both Earth and the Moon were pelted by comets and asteroids shortly after they formed. On the virtually airless Moon (*opposite*), the craters left by this bombardment remained more or less unchanged for billions of years. Most of the craters on Earth, however, were erased as a result of volcanic activity and erosion by the atmosphere and oceans.

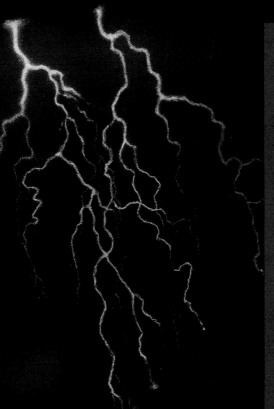

A fiery object from space strikes Earth as a dinosaur watches.

Visitors from Space

Earth has long been visited by countless objects from space. Most of them burn up harmlessly in our atmosphere as fiery meteors. A few scientists have even suggested that Earth is under daily bombardment by thousands of mini-comets. These mini-comets, over billions of years, would have "flown in" enough water to fill Earth's oceans.

Sometimes Earth is hit by a sizable meteorite or comet. Most scientists believe that a comet or asteroid that struck Earth around 65 million years ago led to the extinction of the dinosaurs. There is a crater about 3/4 mile (1.2 km) wide in Arizona where a large meteorite may have struck 50,000 years ago. In 1908, a small comet or asteroid may have exploded in the atmosphere above Siberia, knocking down a forest of trees. If events like these had taken place at or near a city, millions of people could have lost their lives.

On Earth, craters formed by large impacts are slowly filled in by the action of wind, water, and volcanoes. On airless worlds, like the Moon, the craters remain intact through time.

Left: Countless craters exist on the Moon, shown here in a south-pole view.

What killed the dinosaurs?

It was 65 million years ago that dinosaurs vanished from Earth. When scientists dig up rocks that are 65 million years old, they find unusual amounts of the rare metal iridium. This may have come from an object striking Earth. Most scientists now believe that a comet or asteroid strike caused the dinosaurs to die out. In the future, could such a strike wipe out other forms of life, including humans? Perhaps by then we will have the technology to predict such an event and take precautions.

Fact File: Halley's Comet Through the Ages

Not all ancient peoples were mystified and frightened by comets. For example, the ancient Babylonians suspected that comets were celestial bodies like planets or groups of stars. And by the 1400s to 1500s, European astronomers began treating comets calmly as astronomical phenomena.

In the late seventeenth century, Edmond Halley had an idea that has affected people's thinking about comets to this very day.

He believed that comets travel in elliptical, or oval, paths similar to those of the planets. This meant that comets could be tracked and their Earthly visits calculated and even predicted.

Halley used Newton's Law of Gravity to accurately predict the return of the comet that was eventually named after him. The chart on the next page shows other notable sightings of Halley's comet - perhaps the world's favorite and most famous comet.

Below and opposite: **Throughout history, Halley's Comet has been "captured" in various images.**

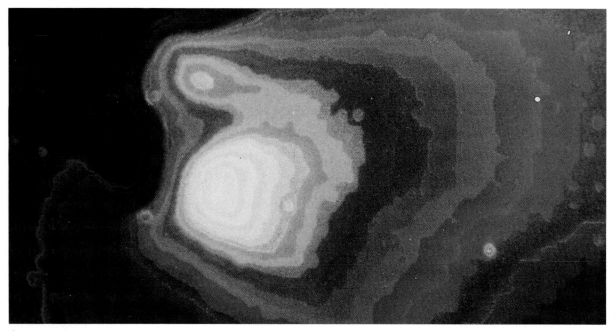

Computer-generated image, 1986.

240 B.C. First recorded sighting of Halley's Comet, by Chinese as a "hairy" or "broom" star. After this date, every appearance of Halley on its 75-76 year course has been recorded.

164 B.C. Observation recorded on a Babylonian tablet discovered in 1985.

11 B.C. While the birth of Christ is said to have occurred eleven years later, some historians believe that perhaps the birth took place at this time and that the famous Star of Bethlehem may have been Halley's Comet.

A.D. 66 Mentioned in Chinese records. Interpreted as foretelling the destruction of the Temple of Jerusalem by Rome four years later in A.D. 70.

141-374 This is the time of the Roman Empire, but neither the Romans nor the Greeks were as interested in astronomy as the Chinese, so sightings during this period are mentioned in Chinese records only.

684 The comet is represented in the form of a woodcut in Germany. The comet was supposed to have predicted catastrophic storms, a poor harvest, and plague.

837 Best recorded view from Earth to date. Mentioned only in Chinese records. Comes within 5 million miles (8 million km) of Earth. Interpreted to have foretold the death, three years later, of an emperor.

1066 Thought to have foretold the defeat of Harold of England by William the Conqueror of Normandy.

1456 At the request of the pope, Europeans pray against it as an evil omen. Seen as a heavenly comment on the fall of Constantinople to the Turks three years before.

1682 Noted by Edmond Halley, who uses prior sightings and Newton's Law of Gravity to predict the next arrival for 1758.

1759 Halley's first predicted arrival. It is one year later than the original estimate because the comet passes close to the strong gravitational pull of the planet Jupiter.

1835 Thanks in part to astronomers' abilities to predict its arrival, Halley's Comet is enjoyed by many people for the first time. Their fear is replaced by curiosity.

1910 Halley's Comet is examined scientifically and considered not dangerous to beings on Earth. Even so, people buy special pills as protection against the imagined poisonous effects of the comet. At this sighting, the tail stretches across much of the sky.

1986 In some ways, a disappointing sighting. The comet spent its brightest time farthest away from Earth, so it looked relatively faint when it reached its closest distance to Earth on April 10. But thanks to modern methods of gathering information, including space probes sent from Earth to meet Halley, astronomers gathered exciting information about Halley and comets in general. This was also an important sighting in other ways because it involved international scientific cooperation.

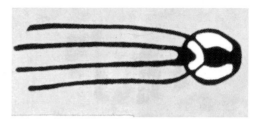

Chinese painting on silk, 168 B.C.

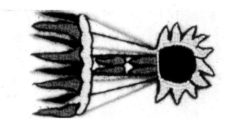

French tapestry, 1066.

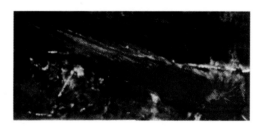

Italian painting by artist Giotto, 1300s.

Polish illustration, 1600s.

Photograph, 1910.

More Books about Comets and Meteors

Asteroids. Isaac Asimov (Gareth Stevens)

Asteroids, Comets, and Meteorites: Cosmic Invaders of the Earth. Jon Erickson (Facts on File)

Asteroids, Comets, and Meteors. Robin Kerrod (Lerner)

Comets and Asteroids: Ice and Rocks in Space. Michael D. Cole (Enslow)

Killer Rocks from Outer Space: Asteroids, Comets, and Meteors. Steven N. Koppes (Carolrhoda)

A Look at Comets. Ray Spangenburg and Kit Moser (Franklin Watts)

Meteors, Meteorites, and Meteoroids. Ray Spangenburg, Kit Moser, and Diane Moser (Franklin Watts)

CD-ROM

Comet Explorer. (Cyanogen)

Web Sites

The Internet is a good place to get more information about comets and meteors. The web sites listed here can help you learn about the most recent discoveries, as well as those made in the past.

American Meteor Society, Gary W. Kronk. comets.amsmeteors.org/

European Space Agency. www.esa.int/

NASA, Comet Observation Home Page. encke.jpl.nasa.gov/index.html

Nine Planets. www.nineplanets.org/

Views of the Solar System. www.solarviews.com/eng/homepage.htm

Places to Visit

Here are some museums and centers where you can learn more about comets and meteors.

Adler Planetarium and Astronomy Museum
1300 S. Lake Shore Drive
Chicago, IL 60605-2403

American Museum of Natural History
Rose Center for Earth and Space
Central Park West at 79th Street
New York, NY 10024

Meteor Crater Visitor Center
Interstate 40, Exit 233
Winslow, AZ 86047

Museum of Science, Boston
Science Park
Boston, MA 02114

National Air and Space Museum
Smithsonian Institution
6th and Independence Avenue SW
Washington, DC 20560

Scienceworks Museum
2 Booker Street
Spotswood, Melbourne, Victoria 3015
Australia

Glossary

asteroids: very small "planets." More than a million of them exist in our Solar System. Most of them orbit the Sun between Mars and Jupiter.

astronomer: a person involved in the scientific study of the Universe and its various celestial bodies.

atmosphere: gases surrounding a planet, star, or moon.

centaurs: asteroid-like bodies found between Jupiter and Nepune that may have escaped from the Kuiper Belt. Some also have comet-like features.

comet: an object in space made of ice, rock, and dust. When its orbit brings it closer to the Sun, it develops a hazy "coma" around its core as well as a tail of gas and dust.

crater: a hole or pit on a planet or similar celestial body that was created by a volcanic explosion or the impact of a meteorite or asteroid.

evaporation: the turning of water into a vapor or gas.

gravity: the force that causes objects like Earth and the Moon to be drawn to one another.

Halley's Comet: a comet that passes by Earth every 75-76 years. It was named for English astronomer Edmond Halley. Every visit by this comet has been documented since its first definite recorded sighting by the Chinese in 240 B.C. Its last pass by Earth occurred in 1986, when it became the first comet to be photographed up-close by spacecraft.

Kuiper Belt: region of the Solar System that exends beyond the orbit of Neptune and contains numerous icy and rocky bodies. It is the source of many comets.

meteor: a meteoroid that has entered Earth's atmosphere. Also, the bright streak of light made as the meteoroid enters or moves through the atmosphere.

meteor shower: a concentrated group of meteors, visible when the Earth's orbit intersects debris from a comet.

meteorite: a meteoroid when it strikes Earth.

meteoroid: a lump of rock or metal drifting through space. Meteoroids can be as big as asteroids or as small as specks of dust.

NASA: the space agency of the United States - the National Aeronautics and Space Administration.

Oort Cloud: a grouping of comets in the outermost reaches of the Solar System. It is named after Dutch astronomer Jan Oort, who suggested its existence in 1950.

orbit: the path that one celestial object follows as it circles, or revolves around, another.

probe: a craft that travels in space, photographing and gathering data about celestial bodies, and in some cases even landing on them.

"shooting star": a meteor that appears as a temporary streak of light in the night sky.

Solar System: the Sun with the planets and all the other bodies, such as asteroids and comets, that orbit it.

Sun: Earth's star and the provider of the energy that makes life on Earth.

vapor: a gas formed from a solid or liquid. On Earth, clouds are made from water vapor.

Index

Born in 1920, Isaac Asimov came to the United States as a young boy from his native Russia. As a young man, he was a student of biochemistry. In time, he became one of the most productive writers the world has ever known. His books cover a spectrum of topics, including science, history, language theory, fantasy, and science fiction. His brilliant imagination gained him the respect and admiration of adults and children alike. Sadly, Isaac Asimov died shortly after the publication of the first edition of *Isaac Asimov's Library of the Universe*.

The publishers wish to thank the following for permission to reproduce copyright material: front cover, 3, 17 (large), © Mark Paternostro; 4 (large) © Dennis Milon; 4 (inset), NASA/JPL; 5, © Keith Ward 1989; 6, NASA Kennedy Space Center; 7 (large), 11 (upper), 23, Mary Evans Picture Library; 7 (inset), © Alan McClure; 8 (left), 9 (lower), Jet Propulsion Laboratory, International Halley Watch; 8 (right), Courtesy Harold Reitsema, Ball Aerospace Systems Division/© 1986 Max Planck Institute; 9 (upper), Max Planck Institute, West Germany; 9 (lower), Jet Propulsion Laboratory, International Halley Watch; 10, Neg. #282680, Courtesy Department of Library Services, American Museum of Natural History; 11 (lower) © Gareth Stevens, Inc., 1989; 12, 16, 28, NASA; 13 (upper), © William K. Hartmann; 13 (lower), NASA and M. Brown (Caltech); 14, © Julian Baum 1988; 15, © Mark Maxwell 1989; 17 (inset), © Garret Moore 1987; 18, © Michael Carroll; 19, © David Milon; 20, 21 (inset), © Edward J. Olsen; 21 (large), Matthew Groshek/© Gareth Stevens, Inc., 1989; 22, Historical Pictures Services, Chicago; 24, Naval Research Laboratory; 25 (large), © Paul Dimare 1987; 25 (inset), Jet Propulsion Laboratory; 26 (large), © Bruce Bond; 26 (inset), © Julian Baum; 27, NASA; 29 (all), © Anne Norcia 1985.